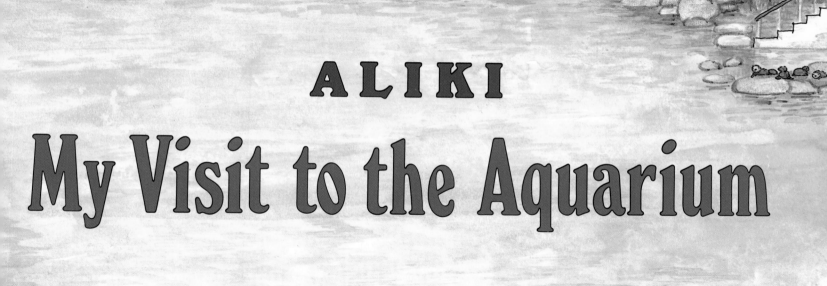

ALIKI

My Visit to the Aquarium

HarperCollins*Publishers*

The aquarium in this book is invented, but it is based on several actual aquariums.

Many thanks to many people for their help, their knowledge, and their enthusiasm.
Here are some of them:

David M. Pittenger *(National Aquarium in Baltimore)*, Twig, Rebecca, and Katie.

Jack Cover and Bruce Hecker *(National Aquarium in Baltimore)*, Steven Webster *(Monterey Bay Aquarium)*,

John Hewitt *(Aquarium of the Americas, New Orleans)*, Judith L. Wellington *(New Jersey State Aquarium)*,

Kate Morgan Jackson, Heather Henson, Barbara Fenton, Christine Kettner, Denise Rennis, Judith Downie, William C. Morris,
Jennifer Pasanen, David Tripp, Helen Lambros, Ann and Gregory Liacouras, Erin Sorenson, and Elan Polushko.

The illustrations for this book were done on watercolor board, using a combination of ink, watercolors, and pencil crayons.

My Visit to the Aquarium   Copyright © 1993 by Aliki Brandenberg   Printed in the U.S.A.   All rights reserved.
Typography by Christine Kettner   3   4   5   6   7   8   9   10   ❖

Library of Congress Cataloging-in-Publication Data   My visit to the aquarium / Aliki.   p.   cm.
Summary: During his visit to an aquarium, a boy finds out about the characteristics and
environments of many different marine and freshwater creatures.
ISBN 0-06-021458-9. — ISBN 0-06-021459-7 (lib. bdg.)
1. Aquariums, Public—Juvenile literature.   2. Aquatic biology—Juvenile literature.
[1. Aquariums, Public.   2. Aquatic biology.   3. Marine animals.   4. Freshwater animals.]   I. Title.
QL78.A15   1993   597'.0074—dc20   92-18678   CIP   AC

for
Jim Zeidman
who led me to the sea

Jason Brandenberg
who threw me a line

Kate Nelson, her fifth-grade class, and Doug
who supplied the bait

TODAY I went to the aquarium with my little sister
and my big brother.
The minute we walked in, I knew we'd have fun.

The aquarium is full of fish—and they are all alive!
Some of the fish—and other aquatic creatures—were born right here.
Some were collected from the salty seas and fresh waters where they live.
Here in the aquarium, they swim in their own kind of water,
in their own natural settings.
I found out how they live, just by looking.

We started at the tropical coral reef.
It was like a sunny underwater garden,
busy with bright little fish.
The fish live, hide, and lay their eggs in the nooks
and chambers of the porous stony coral.

Other creatures live on the reef, too.
We saw stiff lacy sea fans, brittle sponges, soft coral,
and flower-like anemones waving in the water.
Though they look like plants, they are all animals.

We saw beautiful fish with funny names.
Some fish were disguised by colorful camouflage.
Other fish can't tell if they are coming or going—
and neither could I.

lookdown fish

bannerfish

trigger fish

emperor angelfish

four-eyed butterfly fish

blue-ringed angelfish

blue chromis

There were busy fish that never stopped working.
Some poked around for food with their long noses.

beaked coralfish

long-nosed butterfly fish

A parrotfish with strong,
beak-like teeth broke off coral
to find food inside.

parrotfish

scribbled angelfish

semicircle angelfish

blowfish

jawfish

A blowfish puffed up for protection,
and jawfish buried themselves in sand.

We saw fish cleaning other fish.

cleaner wrasse

porkfish

Clownfish live safely in anemones,
which would sting and eat
any other fish.

scorpion fish

One dangerous character looks like a rock—
but it can snap up an unsuspecting fish.
And another has poisonous spines.

lionfish

In separate tanks, we saw seahorses that live in coastal waters.
A seahorse doesn't look or swim like a fish, but it is one.
We saw jellyfish—delicate marine animals from the open sea.
We saw crustaceans—crabs and a lobster—that live on rocky reefs.
So does the octopus, which changes color to hide itself.
It is a mollusk, which has a soft body and no backbone.

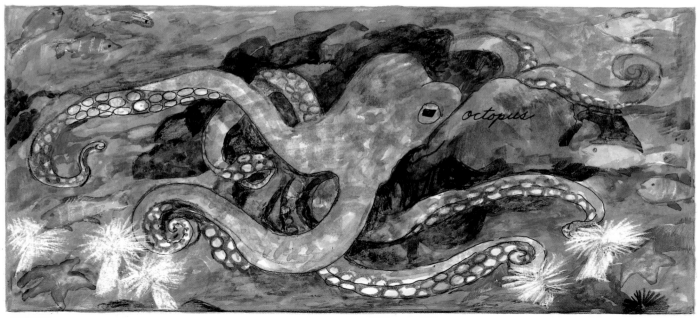

Down the hall, we saw penguins—those funny seabirds.
My sister said they look like little people waddling around in suits.
Penguins don't fly, but they are speedy swimmers.
We saw them chasing little fish, but they couldn't catch one.

We passed anchovies, which like to swim close together.
There were hundreds and hundreds of them, packed in tight,
moving in never-ending circles.

Then we came to the giant kelp forest.
It was three stories high, and teeming with life.
Here fish lay their eggs and graze on tiny creatures
that live in the kelp.

Fish of all sizes swarmed around the swaying kelp plants.
High in the sunlight, schools of sardines moved as one silver cloud.
Below, bottom fish brushed the sandy floor, and eels slid behind rocks.
They share their cool space with crustaceans, mollusks, and starfish.

leopard shark

blacksmith

garibaldi

wolf-eel

It was feeding time.
The smaller fish darted up for food, sprinkled from above.
Just then, a diver swam in to feed the big ones
from a bag of fish.
Hungry mouths opened and snapped shut.
I could see the shark's teeth.
In an aquarium, fish are fed carefully and enough,
so they will not be tempted to eat each other.

rockfish

treefish

moray eel

sheephead

ling cod

In nature, many fish eat other fish.
Others eat tiny floating creatures called plankton.
Bottom fish find worms and crabs in the sand.
Some bottom fish are scavengers—they eat what other fish drop.
The diver finished, and he waved as he left.

We ran upstairs to my brother's favorite hall.
My sister grabbed my hand.
The room was dark, and full of sharks!
This was the hall of the cold open sea, where fish
have space to grow big.
The sharks were huge, and there were all kinds.

sevengill shark

sixgill shark

striped bass

dogfish shark

copper rockfish

As they zoomed past, I almost forgot they were
behind a thick window.
There were other big fish, too.
Some skimmed along the bottom, where flat flounders
and skates were half buried in sand.

leopard shark

sandtiger shark

flounder

skate

After that, we had fun at the tide pool.
The tide pool creatures live among rocks and seaweed
along the seacoast, where tides rise and fall.
They need water to live, but many can survive out of it for a while.
We held starfish, and I touched nearly everything—
except the crab.

We tried to catch the bat rays, gliding like pancakes
in their own shallow pool.
Rays, sharks, and skates are the only fishes without bones
in their bodies.
They have soft cartilage skeletons.

After some lunch, we walked on.
It was muggy in the tropical rain forest.
A parrot squawked in the dense trees.

neon tetra

pacu

piranha

crested forest lizard

scarlet ibis

anaconda

red-eyed tree frog

Living things thrive in this hot, misty climate.
In fact, half of all the world's wildlife species live in rain forests.
We saw tiny neon tetras, pacu, and a piranha with razor-sharp teeth.
We saw birds and lizards, snakes, turtles, and frogs.

yellow perch

catfish

killifish

snapping turtle

sturgeon

Next we saw perch and catfish with whiskers
and fishes of all kinds that live in fresh water.
They crowd lakes, rivers, swamps, and streams.

Turtles and other reptiles share the leafy habitat.
A floating alligator peeked out of the murky water.
Reptiles need air and water to live.

In the coastal stream exhibit, we saw fish that travel.
They live in fresh and salt water, and in semisalted
coastal streams that lead to the sea.

COASTAL STREAM

Salmon and trout are marine creatures.
Salmon live mostly in the sea, and so do many trout.
But every year, these fish migrate to freshwater streams
to lay their eggs.
They have to swim hard against currents to get there.

At the beach environment, seabirds raced with the tide.
Some jabbed their long beaks into wet sand.
They looked for something to eat along the shell-scattered shore.

From an outside terrace, we could see
the marine mammals that live in the bay.
Friendly sea otters frolicked and floated
as they fed on sea urchins, crabs, and clams.
Beyond them, slippery seals flapped
on their rocks.

Then came the biggest treat of all—the dolphins and beluga whales.
What a rumpus they made! They leaped and dove, whistled and splashed,
showing off in their big new pool.

Dolphins and belugas seem to smile,
and their little teeth show when they do.
Before we left, a beluga came close to say goodbye.

What a great day it was.
Think of it. We were in tide pools, coastal streams,
coral reefs, deep seas, and splashing rivers.
And we only got our hands wet!

ALL the living things in this book are at risk. They are endangered by people who pollute, litter, and destroy the earth.

- Every year, thousands of sea creatures are killed by plastic garbage—containers, bags, and balloons—that litters beaches and waters. All this litter could be recycled.

- Every day, paint, oil, gasoline, and chemicals are sprayed into the air and spilled into water. One such gallon pollutes 750,000 gallons of water—and endangers the creatures in it. These poisons pollute the air, too. They have changed our weather and are destroying our ozone layer.

- Every day, hunters and poachers kill animals for tusks, skins, or sport.

- Every day, over one hundred wildlife species become extinct.

- Every second, one acre of tropical rain forest is destroyed for land and trees. In that second, people and wildlife become homeless, and many creatures die.

We can all help to change things. Many caring groups know what to do. Join them. Remember, this is our world, too.